WELCOME

Since their debut almost a decade ago, TWICE has become one of the most beloved K-pop girl groups. They have explored almost every concept, from bubblegum pop to girl crush, sold millions of albums, racked up billions of streams, and toured stadiums around the world. With this ultimate fan's guide, you can discover everything you need to know to become a true ONCE, from profiles of each member to an exploration of their discography, and four stunning pull-out posters!

ULTIMATE FAN'S GUIDE TO **TWICE**

Nayeon

Nayeon, AKA Im Na-yeon, is a lead vocalist in TWICE, as well as a dancer. Born on 22 September 1995 in Seoul, South Korea, Nayeon secretly auditioned for JYP Entertainment – despite her mother forbidding it – and became a trainee in 2010. She trained for five years before competing in the reality show *SIXTEEN* and becoming a member of TWICE. The singer also boasts a successful solo career and her debut album, *Im Nayeon*, was the first one by a solo South Korean artist to reach the top ten on the *Billboard* 200.

"Nayeon secretly auditioned for JYP Entertainment – despite her mother forbidding it"

ULTIMATE FAN'S GUIDE TO **TWICE**

"Jeongyeon auditioned to join JYP Entertainment as a child, eventually succeeding in March 2010"

Jeongyeon

Yoo Jeong-yeon, AKA Jeongyeon, is another lead vocalist for TWICE. Born Yoo Kyung-wan, a year after Nayeon, on 1 November 1996, Jeongyeon grew up with two siblings in Suwon, South Korea. Jeongyeon auditioned to join JYP Entertainment as a child, eventually succeeding in March 2010. She was initially due to join a JYP group with Nayeon, Sana and Jihyo, but after the project was cancelled, she participated in *SIXTEEN* to join TWICE. With her sister, the actress Gong Seung-yeon, Jeongyeon hosted the 2016 SBS Entertainment Awards, for which she won the Best New Female Talent award.

"*Momo is the main dancer, sub vocalist and sub rapper of the group*"

Momo

Momo Hirai was born in Kyoto, Japan, on 9 November 1996. Momo is the main dancer, sub vocalist and sub rapper of the group. After JYP Entertainment saw a video of her and her sister dancing, she was scouted to audition in 2011, where she succeeded in becoming a JYP trainee. Momo was a trainee for around three years before she became a member of TWICE, and she is widely considered to be one of the best dancers in the world of K-pop. In 2023, Momo teamed up with Sana and Mina to form the sub-unit MiSaMo, debuting with the EP *Masterpiece*.

ULTIMATE FAN'S GUIDE TO TWICE

Sana

Sana Minatozaki was born in 29 December 1996 in Osaka, Japan. Another member of the sub-unit MiSaMo, Sana is known for her vocals in TWICE and she often sings the really catchy – and viral – parts of their songs. Before she was scouted by JYP Entertainment in a shopping mall, Sana was training to be a singer in Japan with EXPG. In 2012, alongside Momo, Sana was due to become a member of a four-person girl group, but plans were cancelled after South Korean and Japanese tensions grew following the Liancourt Rocks territorial dispute. Sana was also the first TWICE member to release her own solo single, a cover of 'Sotsugyou' originally by Japanese band Kobukuro. She is also an ambassador for several brands including YSL and Graff.

"Sana was due to become a member of a four-person girl group, but plans were cancelled"

ULTIMATE FAN'S GUIDE TO TWICE

Jihyo

Born Park Ji-soo, Park Ji-hyo was born in Gyeonggi Province, South Korea, on 1 February 1997. Jihyo joined JYP Entertainment when she was just eight years old. She trained for ten years, was the face of a teen clothing line with the band Boyfriend for Innisfree, and trained with K-pop artists such as Sunmi, Hyerim, Bae Suzy, Jo Kwon and Nichkhun. Jihyo changed her name to Park Ji-hyo before entering the contest *SIXTEEN* to find the members of TWICE. Jihyo is the main vocalist and heads up the K-pop group as the powerhouse singer of the band. She's highly rated among critics for her incredible vocal range.

"Jihyo is the main vocalist and heads up the K-pop group as the powerhouse singer of the band"

Mina

Mina Myoi was born in San Antonio, Texas, on 24 March 1997 to Japanese expatriates. When she was a toddler, the family moved back to Japan. She was scouted while shopping in Osaka with her mother, which led to her move to South Korea for training by JYP Entertainment in 2014. Alongside Momo, she is a key dancer for the group and known for her elegant style, no doubt honed by her years training in ballet. Mina is also a sub-vocalist for TWICE, debuting in the group with their first EP, *The Story Begins*. A dual citizen of America and Japan by birth, Mina relinquished her American citizenship in 2019 as Japan does not permit dual nationalities.

"She was scouted while shopping in Osaka with her mother, which led to her move to South Korea"

ULTIMATE FAN'S GUIDE TO **TWICE**

"A YouTube video of Dahyun dancing in elementary school at her church drove her to early fame"

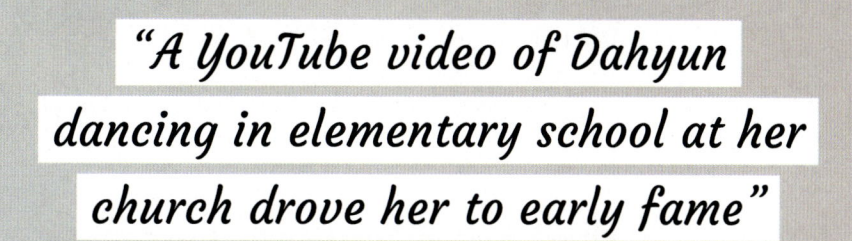

Dahyun

Kim Da-hyun was born in Seongnam, Gyeonggi, on 28 May 1998. Her start in music came from singing with her Christian church choir growing up. A YouTube video of Dahyun dancing in elementary school at her church drove her to early fame, and she was soon recruited by JYP Entertainment after a scout watched her perform at a dance festival. She's now the lead rapper and sub-vocalist of TWICE. In 2024, Dahyun entered the acting industry, as it was announced that she'd be in the film *Sprint*. The same year, she was cast in a Korean remake of the film *You Are the Apple of My Eye*.

"She was involved in the entertainment industry at a young age, modelling for a children's magazine"

Chaeyoung

Son Chae-young, known as Chaeyoung, was born in Seoul, South Korea, on 23 April 1999. She was involved in the entertainment industry at a young age, modelling for a children's magazine. She later took an interest in singing and took dance lessons for a year. When she was 13, she passed the auditions to join JYP Entertainment and appeared in music videos for the groups Got7's and Miss A's in 2014 and 2015. Chaeyoung was the first in the group to gain writing credits for writing a rap verse on TWICE's cover of J.Y. Park's 'Precious Love' in their 2016 EP *Page Two*.

ULTIMATE FAN'S GUIDE TO **TWICE**

"*Tzuyu has been named the 'Light of Taiwan' by the Taiwanese media for her popularity*"

Tzuyu

Chou Tzu-yu was born on 14 June 1999 in the East District of Tainan, Taiwan. She trained at a dance academy from a young age and was discovered by JYP Entertainment scouts at the Muse Performing Arts Workshop in Tainan. Tzuyu is the lead dancer, sub-vocalist, visual and maknae for the group. She's released multiple solo covers, including 'Me!' by Taylor Swift and 'Christmas Without You' by Ava Max. Tzuyu has been involved in philanthropic work, donating ₩50 million to the South Korean Community Chest to help prevent the spread of COVID-19. Tzuyu has been named the 'Light of Taiwan' by the Taiwanese media for her popularity.

ULTIMATE FAN'S GUIDE TO TWICE

The formation of a supergroup

JYP Entertainment launched the show *SIXTEEN* on 5 May 2015 to find the next big K-pop girl group. *SIXTEEN* was a 'survival' reality show that pitted sixteen contestants against each other to win a coveted spot in the girl group TWICE. The show, presented by Park Jin-Young (JYP), started with seven contestants lined up for the group, and the other nine competing to replace them. The final seven members selected were: Nayeon, Sana, Mina, Jeongyeon, Dahyun, Chaeyoung, and Jihyo. However, JYP threw in a bombshell twist at the end when he announced the group would in fact have nine members, with previously eliminated contestants Tzuyu (the audience's choice) and Momo (JYP's choice) added to the lineup.

"SIXTEEN was a 'survival' reality show that pitted sixteen contestants against each other"

ULTIMATE FAN'S GUIDE TO TWICE

The start of the story

The final episode of *SIXTEEN* aired on 7 July 2015, and TWICE's debut single 'Like Ooh-Ahh' followed hot on its tail on 20 October 2015. The song was chosen as the lead single for their first EP, *The Story Begins*, released on the same day. Three months after the release, the song peaked at number 10 on the Gaon Music Charts, an unusual feat for such a new group. *The Story Begins* features six tracks and debuted at four on the Gaon Music Charts, where it then peaked at number three just two weeks later.

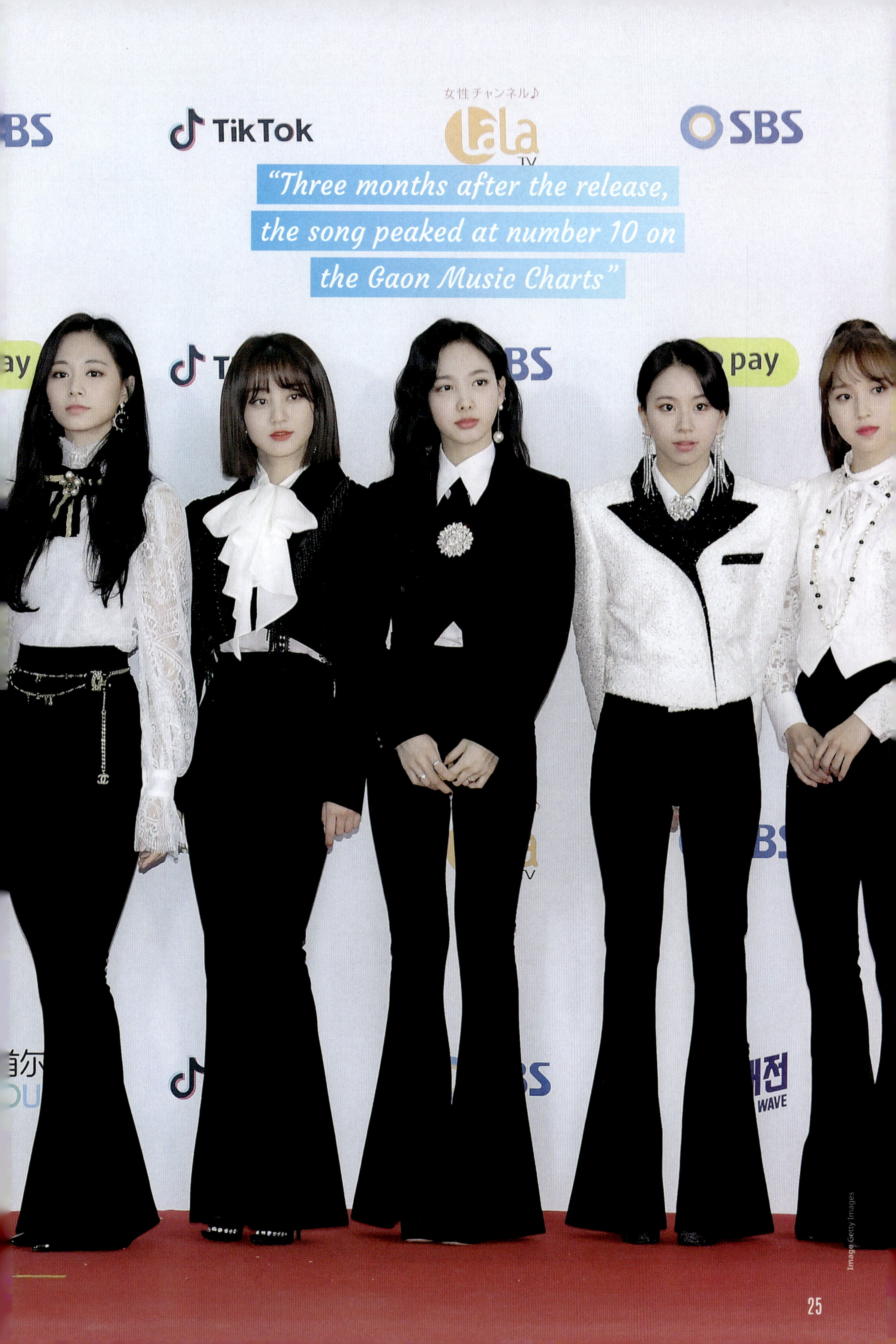

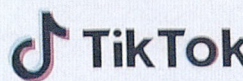

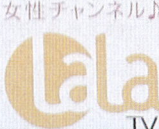

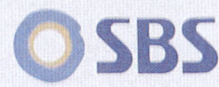

"Three months after the release, the song peaked at number 10 on the Gaon Music Charts"

Image Getty Images

ULTIMATE FAN'S GUIDE TO **TWICE**

ONCE a fan, always a fan

On 4 November 2015, the TWICE members announced the official name of their fan club on Instagram, saying, 'If you love us even once, we'll repay you with TWICE our love', and so ONCE was born. There are two membership types for ONCE; ONCE Candy for Korean members, and ONCE Jelly for those that live outside of Korea. Both memberships grant a membership card and ONCE Special Package. There have been four generations of ONCE, the most recent in 2023. In 2017, ONCE Japan fan club cards became available, with the TWICE members designing all of the club cards that were released.

"If you love us even once, we'll repay you with TWICE our love"

ULTIMATE FAN'S GUIDE TO TWICE

TWICE's second page

Page Two, TWICE's second EP, was released in April 2016. The lead single on the seven-track EP was 'CHEER UP'. The song was a massive hit, bringing in attention from across the world, with a music video that went viral alongside the track. The song was nominated for 12 awards and won eight. The EP's genre is described as dance-pop and pop and was received well by audiences, taking the number two spot on its release in the Gaon Music Charts. They played music shows throughout May 2016, winning eleven music show awards for their performances of 'CHEER UP'.

"The song was a massive hit, bringing in attention from across the world, with a music video that went viral alongside the track"

ULTIMATE FAN'S GUIDE TO TWICE

TWICEcoaster: both lanes

TWICEcoaster: Lane 1 was the group's third EP, and surpassed *Page Two*'s success almost instantly, proving TWICE a force to be reckoned with. It was released on 24 October 2016, just six months after the release of *Page Two*. The lead single off of the EP was 'TT', which topped all eight of the major South Korean charts online as well as the Gaon Music Charts. In February 2017, TWICE released a reissue of the EP called *TWICEcoaster: Lane 2*, which featured a new track, 'KNOCK KNOCK'. The EP made it onto the *Billboard* World Album Charts at number four, whilst 'KNOCK KNOCK' entered the *Billboard* Digital Charts at number five.

"The EP made it onto the Billboard World Album Charts at number four"

The SIGNAL of success

TWICE showed no signs of slowing down, releasing their fourth EP *SIGNAL* on 15 May 2017. The EP's lead single, with the titular name 'Signal', was produced by JYP himself. TWICE members Jihyo and Chaeyoung wrote lyrics for the fifth track 'Eye Eye Eyes'. The EP followed the trend of the previous EPs by the group, surpassing *TWICEcoaster: Lane 1* in its success, as it set a record for the highest number of first day album sales at 42,000 copies. It entered the *Billboard* World Albums and Digital Songs Chart at number three on both.

ULTIMATE FAN'S GUIDE TO **TWICE**

"All three Japanese members of TWICE are credited for improving Japanese-Korean relations by The Chosun Ilbo"

#TWICE in Japan

TWICE announced its Japanese debut in June 2017 with the compilation album *#TWICE*. The album reached number two on the Oricon Albums Chart, which earned it the highest number of first-week album sales by any K-pop artist in two years in Japan. The K-pop group are incredibly successful in Japan, releasing new songs as well as Japanese versions of their popular Korean singles. All three Japanese members of TWICE are credited for improving Japanese-Korean relations by *The Chosun Ilbo*, the biggest daily newspaper in South Korea. A fan favourite track in Japan is 'Doughnut', the ninth of TWICE's Japanese maxi singles, which was released in 2021. With their popularity showing no signs of slowing down, the group released their fifth Japanese studio album, *Dive*, in July 2024.

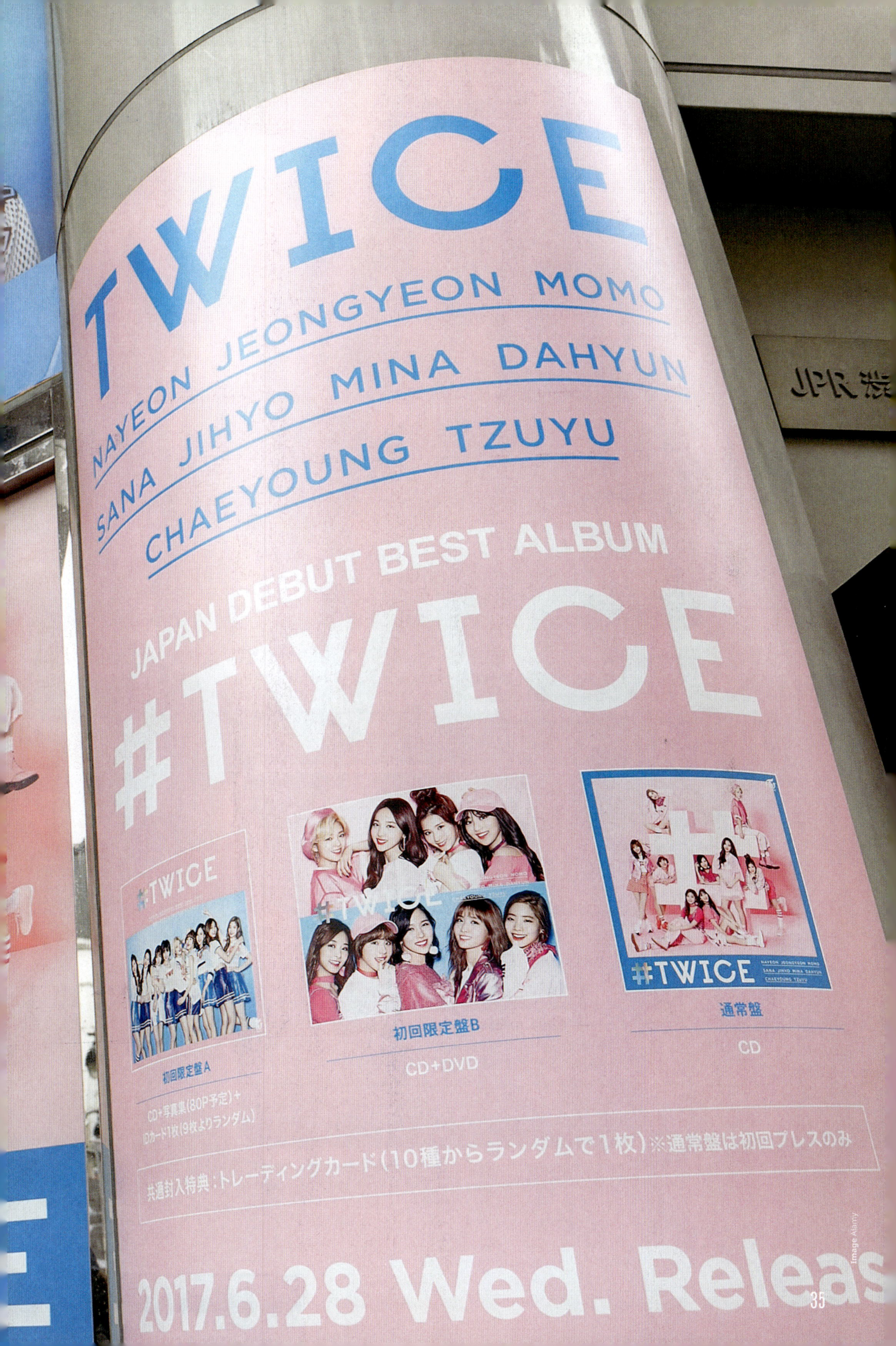
TWICE
NAYEON JEONGYEON MOMO
SANA JIHYO MINA DAHYUN
CHAEYOUNG TZUYU
JAPAN DEBUT BEST ALBUM
#TWICE
初回限定盤A
CD+写真集(80P予定)+
IDカード1枚(9枚よりランダム)
初回限定盤B
CD+DVD
通常盤
CD
共通封入特典：トレーディングカード(10種からランダムで1枚)※通常盤は初回プレスのみ
2017.6.28 Wed. Releas
JPR

Image Alamy

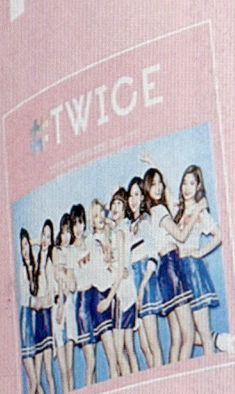

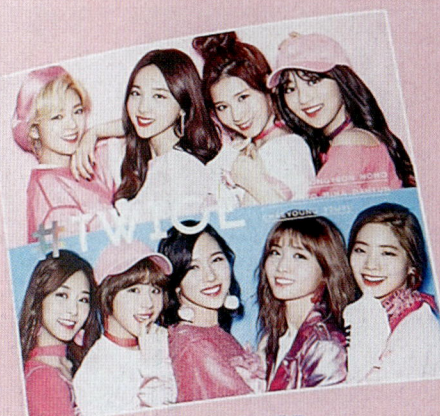

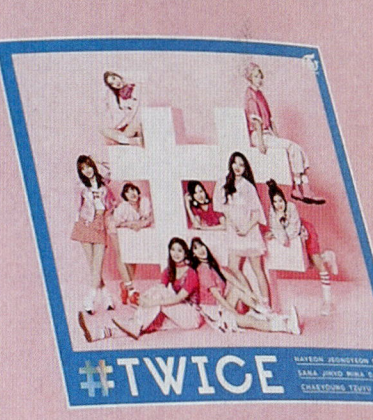

ULTIMATE FAN'S GUIDE TO **TWICE**

The debut studio album

Twicetagram, released on 30 October 2017, marked the debut studio album for the group. It has 13 tracks, the lead single of which is 'Likey'. The track was produced by Black Eyed Pilseung, a South Korean duo who produced 'Like Ooh-Ahh', 'CHEER UP' and 'TT'. The album's genres include pop and dance across the 13 songs. *Billboard* included the album on their '20 Best K-pop Albums of 2017: Critics' Picks'. *Twicetagram* achieved major commercial success, recording over 330,000 pre-orders and achieving number one on the *Billboard* World Album Charts. In December 2017, TWICE released a reissue; *Merry & Happy*, which had the lead single 'Heart Shaker'.

"The album's genres include pop and dance across the 13 songs"

ULTIMATE FAN'S GUIDE TO TWICE

What is Love? & Summer Nights

On 9 April 2018, TWICE released their fifth EP, *What is Love?*, with a lead single of the same name. The EP beat TWICE's previous records, reaching over 350,000 preorder sales. On its release, the EP reached number two on the Gaon Album Chart and the Oricon Album Chart, and number three on the *Billboard* World Album Chart. The success earned TWICE the achievement of becoming the first Korean female act to earn platinum certification from the Korea Music Content Association – and the fifth music act to do so. TWICE expanded and reissued the EP as *Summer Nights* on 9 July 2018, with the lead single 'Dance the Night Away'.

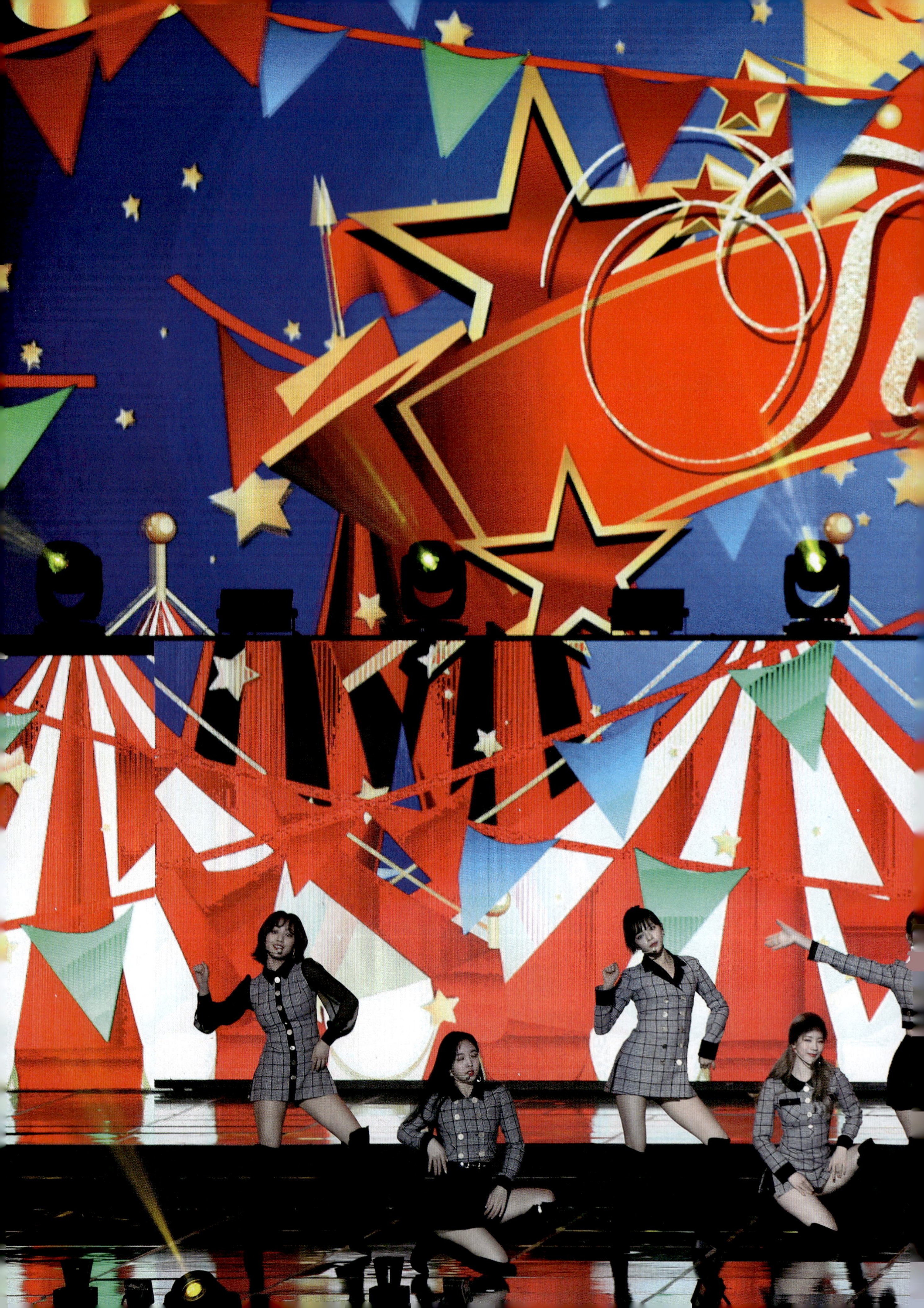

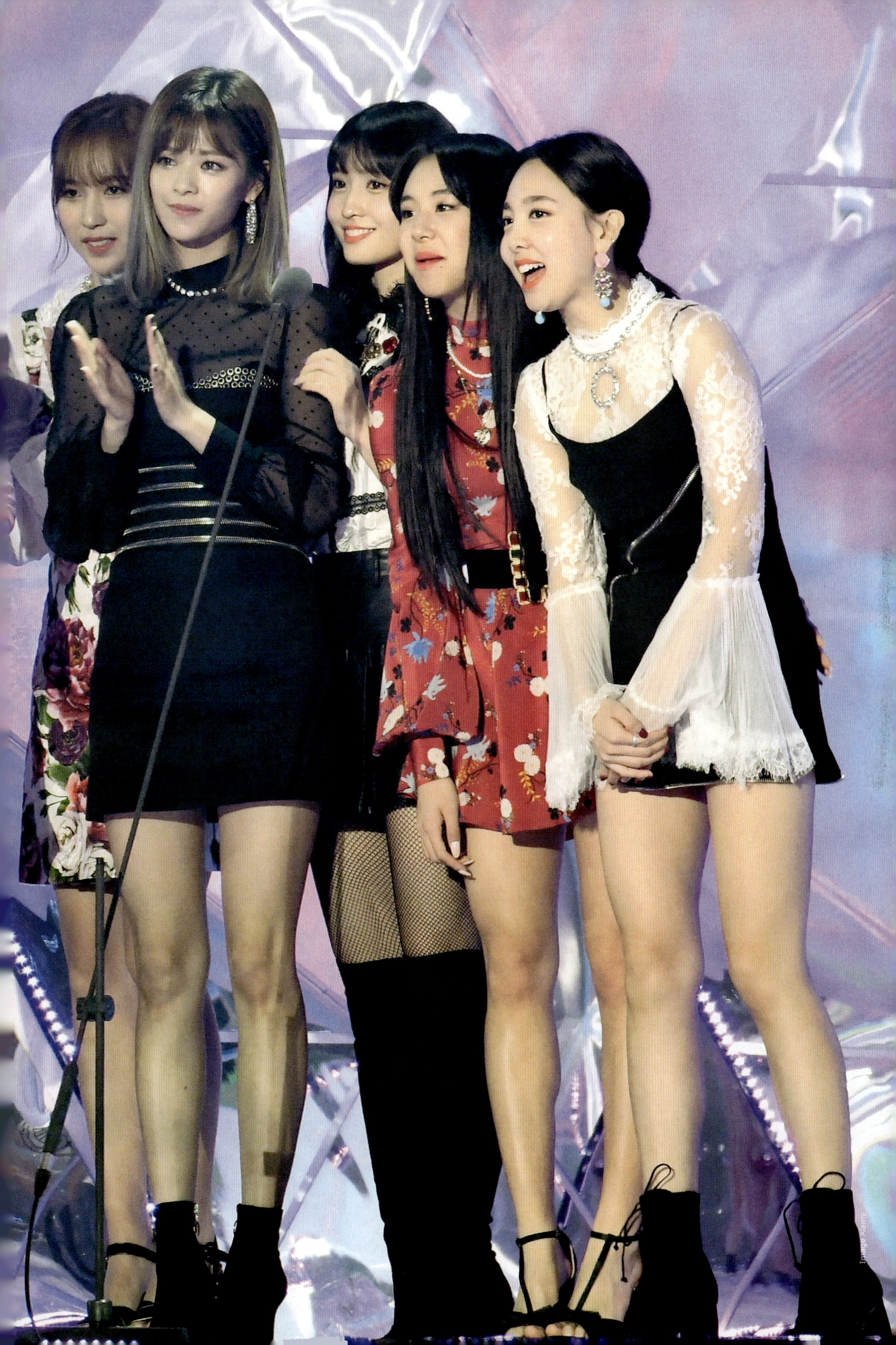

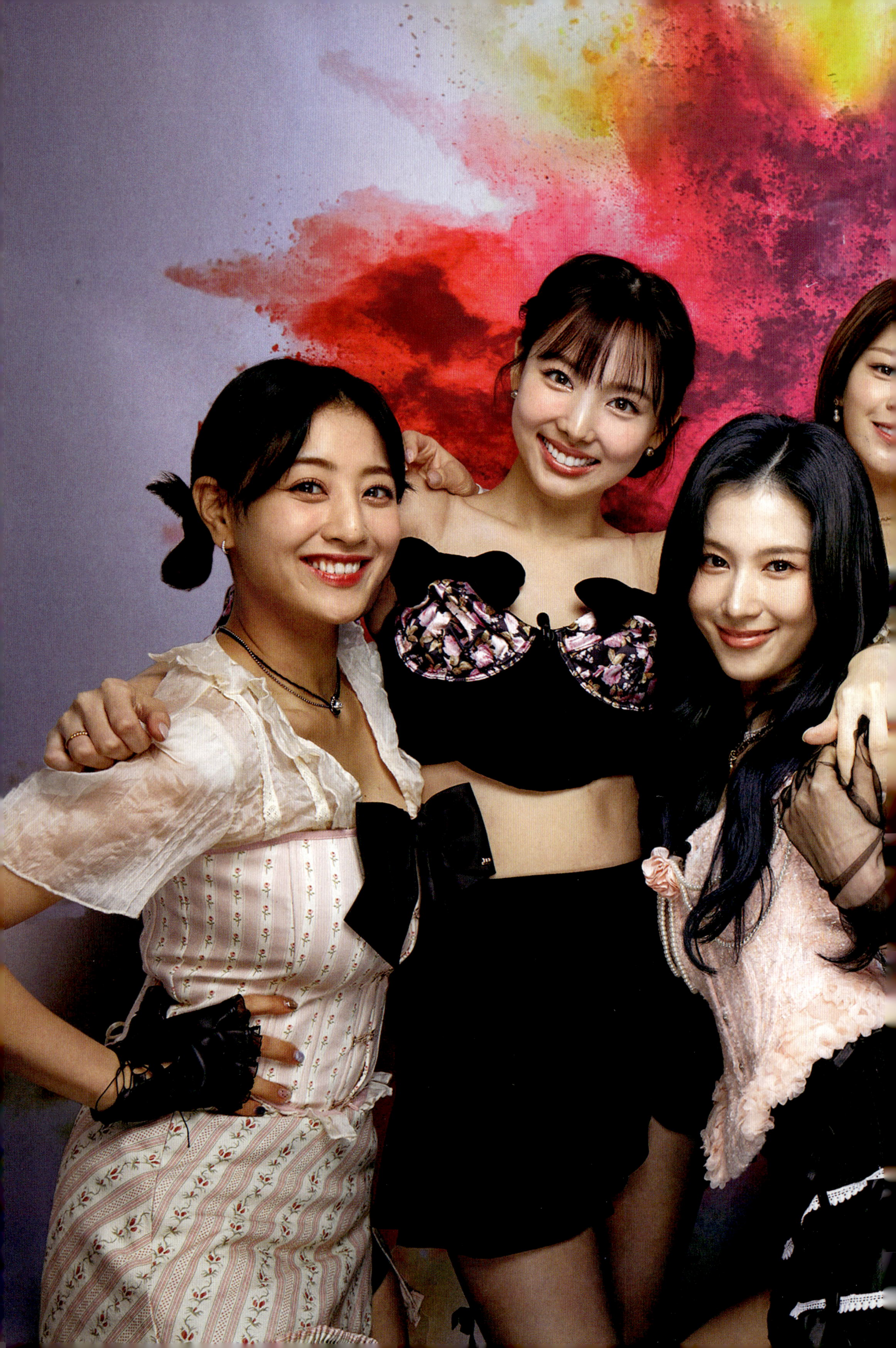

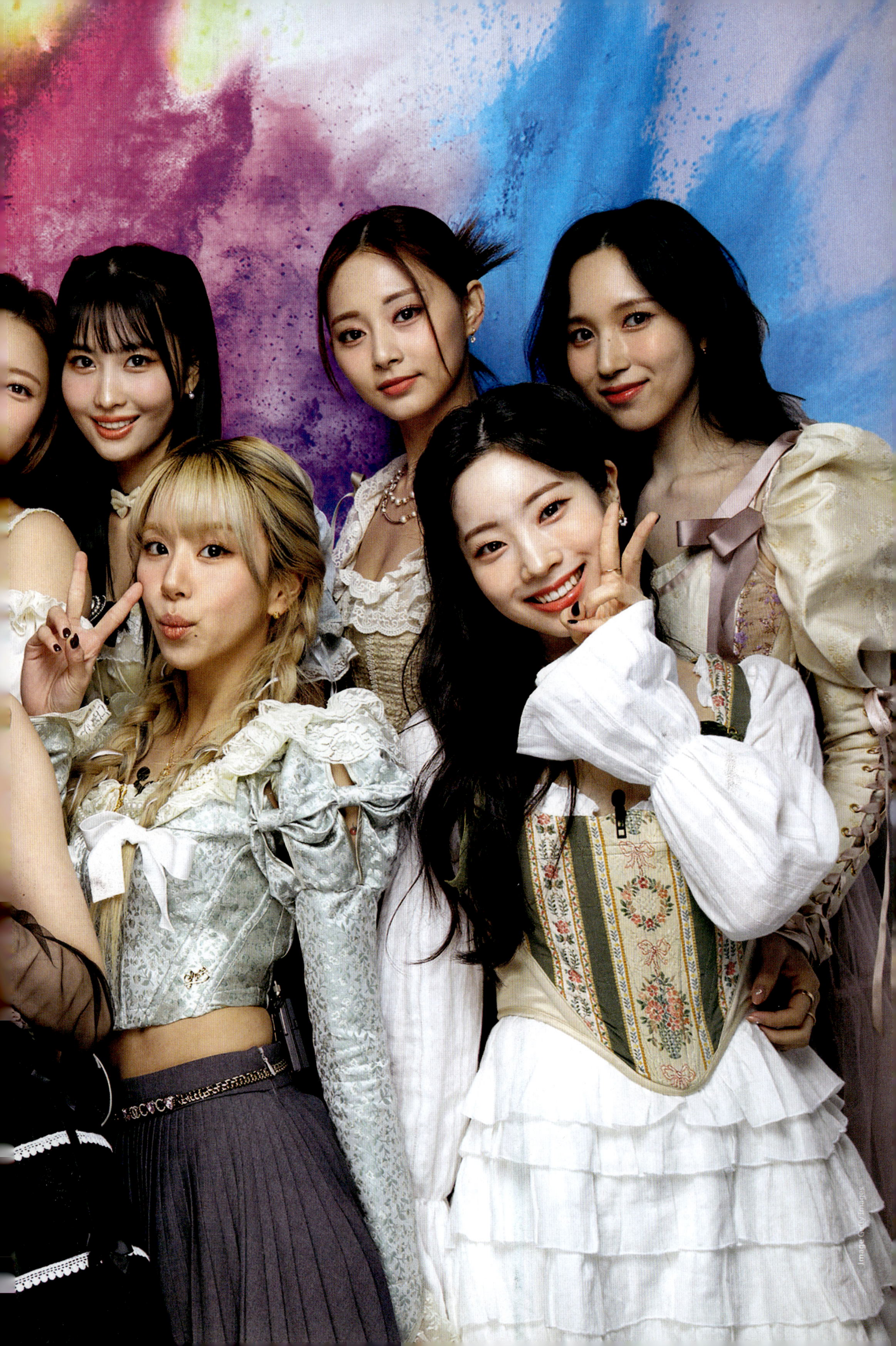

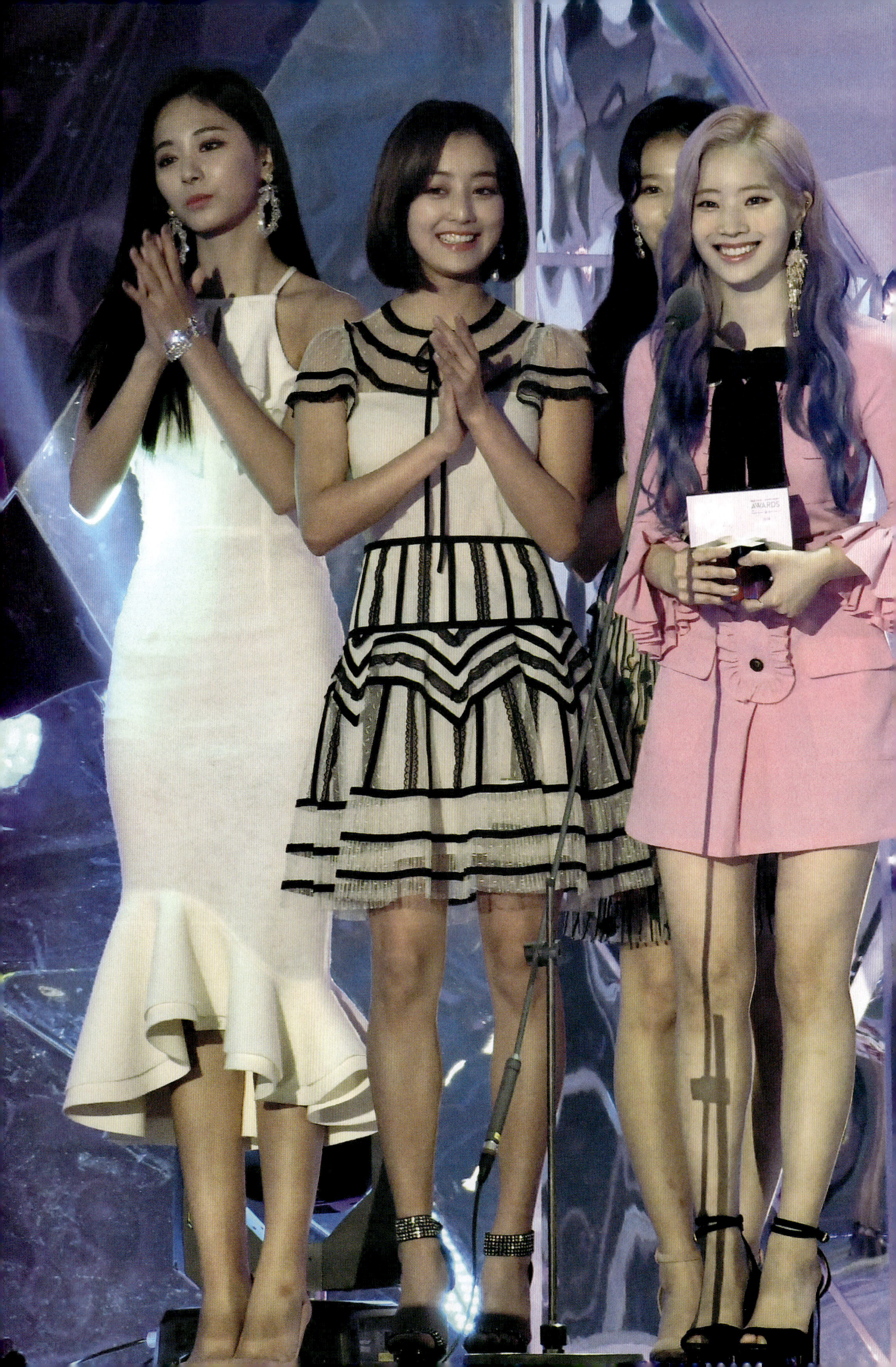
AWARDS

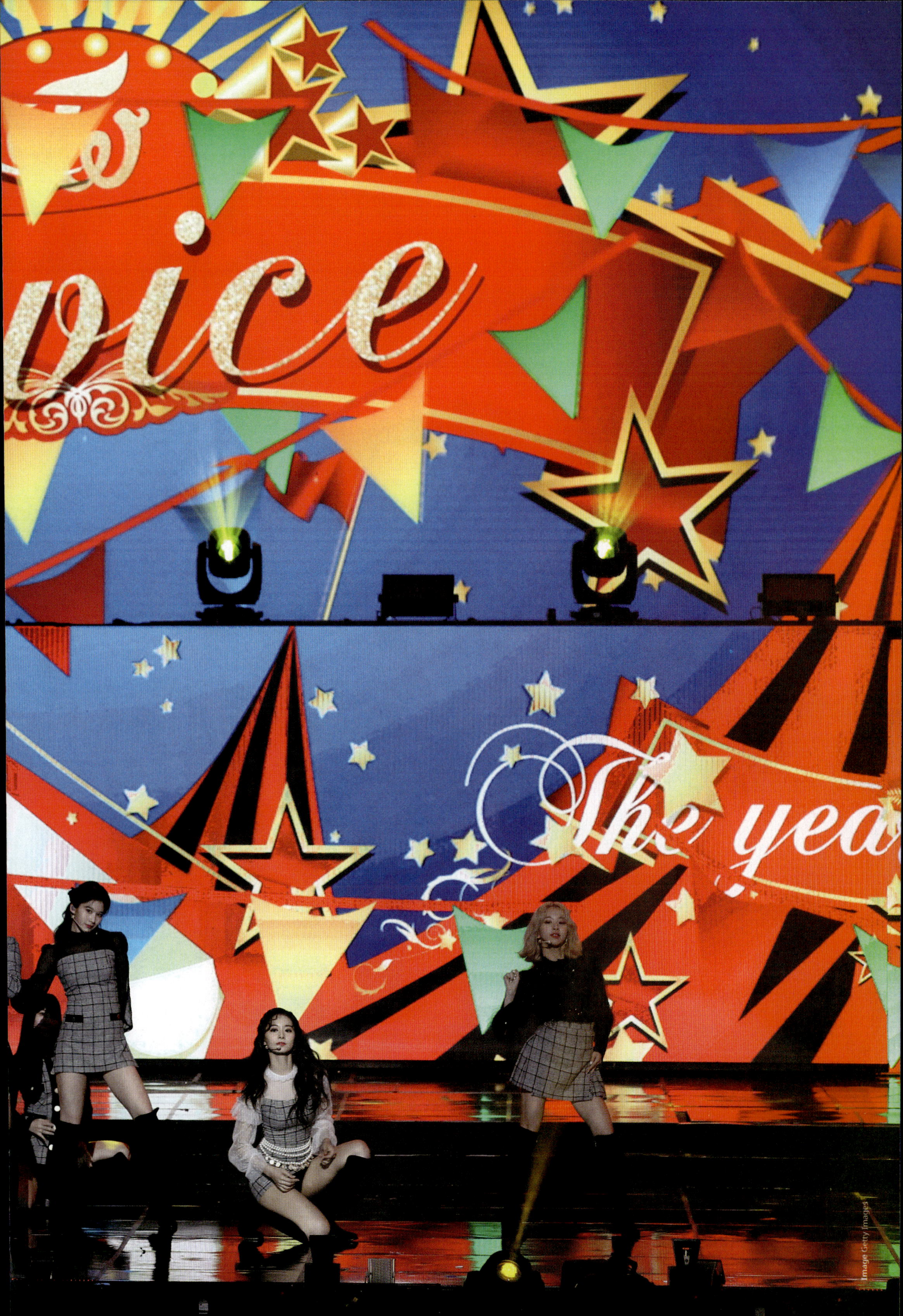

Image Getty Images

YES or YES

The sixth EP from TWICE was *YES or YES*, which includes seven tracks with the title single 'YES or YES' securing the lead spot. It was released on 5 November 2018, and Jihyo, Chaeyoung and Jeongyeon all wrote lyrics for three of the songs. The EP charted at number one on the Gaon Album Chart, and 'YES or YES' made it to number one after the first week on the Digital Charts. They reissued the EP as *The Year of "Yes"* with 'The Best Thing I Ever Did' as the lead single on 12 December 2018.

ULTIMATE FAN'S GUIDE TO **TWICE**

FANCY YOU

FANCY YOU is the seventh EP from TWICE and marks a shift in maturity for the group. They released the EP on 22 April 2019 to their biggest response yet as they beat their record for most sales in the US. The EP follows a girl crush theme; each track reflects the maturity of the girl crush figure and moves away from the cutesy pop of the group's previous EPs. TWICE took on production by Charli XCX, a mainstay in the pop scene, for 'Girls Like Us'. Multiple group members, including Jihyo, all wrote lyrics for this EP.

"Each track reflects the maturity of the girl crush figure and moves away from the cutesy pop of their previous EPs"

ULTIMATE FAN'S GUIDE TO TWICE

8th GAONCHART MUSIC AWARDS 2018

First world tour

TWICE have performed in concerts since 2017, but their first world tour began in May 2019 with the Twicelights World Tour. Before that, the group performed across South Korea and Thailand for the Twiceland opening tour in 2017. In the Twiceland Zone 2: Fantasy Park tour, in 2018, they broadened locations to include Japan and Indonesia. They then toured Japan for the BDZ and #Dreamday tour in 2018 and 2019, respectively. Their first world tour took them across North America to Mexico City, Chicago, Newark and Inglewood. They're currently embarking on their Ready to Be World tour, which takes them as far as Europe and over to Australia.

"They're currently embarking on their Ready to Be World tour, which takes them as far as Europe and over to Australia"

ULTIMATE FAN'S GUIDE TO TWICE

"Some of the biggest endorsements the group have been in include Nike in 2018, and Nintendo in 2021"

Brand ambassadors

TWICE are known for more than just their musical abilities. The members are influencers in their own right, taking on huge partnerships as both a group and as individual members. TWICE teamed up with Pocari Sweat (Ion Water) from 2016 to 2020, appearing in TV commercials that were a hit in Japan. Some of the biggest endorsements the group have been in include Nike in 2018 and Nintendo in 2021. Sana also became a brand ambassador for Prada in 2023, whilst Tzuyu became an ambassador for Crocs Korea. Other major ambassadorships include Momo for Miu Miu Japan and MiSaMo for Google Japan.

POCARI SWEAT

53

ULTIMATE FAN'S GUIDE TO **TWICE**

Feel Special

On 23 September 2019, TWICE released their eighth EP, *Feel Special*. Once again, several of the members took part in writing lyrics across the seven-song tracklist, whilst the lead track 'Feel Special' was written by singer-songwriter Park Jin-young. *Feel Special* beat TWICE's previous records for a best-selling album after its release. The group demonstrated a wide range of musical abilities, featuring EDM and hip-hop in its tracks. The UK garage-influenced 'Rainbow' was written by Nayeon, whilst 'Get Loud' was written by Jihyo, and 'Trick It' was written by Dahyun. Momo wrote the EDM-infused 'Love Foolish'. The final song is the Korean version of 'Breakthrough'.

"The group demonstrated a wide range of musical abilities, featuring EDM and hip-hop in its tracks"

ULTIMATE FAN'S GUIDE TO TWICE

"It marked a further growth in maturity from the group, whilst maintaining their emblematic bright and happy vibe"

MORE & MORE

The ninth EP by TWICE was called *MORE & MORE*, released on 1 June 2020. The group evolved once again as they incorporated new pop styles, including tropical house and Latin pop. The lead track 'MORE & MORE' was composed by some huge names in music, including Zara Larsson and Julia Michaels, and features intimate lyrics about a relationship. Critics rated it highly, and the EP marked a further growth in maturity from the group while maintaining their bright and happy vibe. TWICE smashed their own records with *MORE & MORE*, which made it their new best-selling release.

ULTIMATE FAN'S GUIDE TO **TWICE**

"The album charted once again, proving the group's mettle in R&B and dance-pop"

All eyes on TWICE

Now cemented as a massive K-pop group, TWICE turned their attention to a second Korean studio album, *Eyes Wide Open*. The album was released on 26 October 2020, complete with 13 tracks, the lead single of which was 'I Can't Stop Me'. The album charted well once again, proving the group's mettle in R&B and dance-pop. The album is electric, featuring a range of producers including Park Jin-young, who served as the executive producer. Interestingly, this album has a composition credit for Dua Lipa on the track 'Behind the Mask', which was written by the South Korean artist Heize.

ULTIMATE FAN'S GUIDE TO **TWICE**

Taste of Love

On 11 June 2021, TWICE released *Taste of Love*, their tenth EP. The EP contains six summer bangers, the lead single being 'Alcohol-Free' – an earworm with a particularly catchy guitar riff. Additionally, TWICE released a seventh track, the English version of 'CRY FOR ME', on physical editions. *Taste of Love* received a positive commercial and critical response, which is a routine response for the group to have at this point, with ten EPs under their belt. *Taste of Love* made it to number one on the *Billboard* World Albums Chart, TWICE's second EP to do so.

"The EP contains six summer bangers, the lead single being 'Alcohol-Free'"

ULTIMATE FAN'S GUIDE TO TWICE

The Feels

TWICE released their first official English-language single on 1 October 2021, 'The Feels'. The track ended up becoming the first single on the group's third Korean studio album. The song is classically TWICE: a massive pop hit, and cemented the group's reputation in the English-speaking music industry, with praise from *Rolling Stone* and *Pitchfork* who both included it in their 'Best Of' listicles in 2022. The group got together for a music video, posing as promgoers who eventually perform at the event. 'The Feels' also made it into charts across the world, including the UK, New Zealand, Malaysia and Canada.

"The song cemented TWICE's reputation in the English-speaking music industry, with praise from Rolling Stone and Pitchfork"

ULTIMATE FAN'S GUIDE TO TWICE

"Multiple TWICE members wrote lyrics for the album, including Nayeon; Jihyo; Chaeyoung and Dahyun"

The Formula of Love

Formula of Love: O+T=<3 is the third Korean studio album by TWICE, and the sixth overall. 2021 proved to be a busy year for the group, as the album was released on 12 November 2021, just six months after their tenth EP. The album is features 15 tracks across a variety of genres including dance-pop, hip-hop, trap and R&B. The lead single is 'SCIENTIST', which builds into an explosive dance-pop chorus. Multiple TWICE members wrote lyrics for the album, including Nayeon, Jihyo, Chaeyoung and Dahyun. The album received the highest critical acclaim yet for its cohesiveness, and the roaring success made it into the top spots on charts worldwide.

ULTIMATE FAN'S GUIDE TO TWICE

Nayeon's solo debut

On 24 June 2022, Nayeon released her solo debut EP, *IM NAYEON*. The EP's lead single was 'POP!', a fitting indication of the genre throughout the seven tracks. The EP features Stray Kids star Felix on the slick pop hit 'NO PROBLEM', and South Korean rapper Wonstein on the R&B song 'LOVE COUNTDOWN'. Critics loved the album, describing it as a shift to mature R&B that maintains elements of classic TWICE bubblegum pop; a strong debut for Nayeon. Nayeon's EP both debuted and peaked at number one on the Gaon Album Chart. Nayeon also reached number seven on the US *Billboard* 200.

"Critics loved the album, describing it as a shift to mature R&B that maintains elements of classic TWICE bubblegum pop"

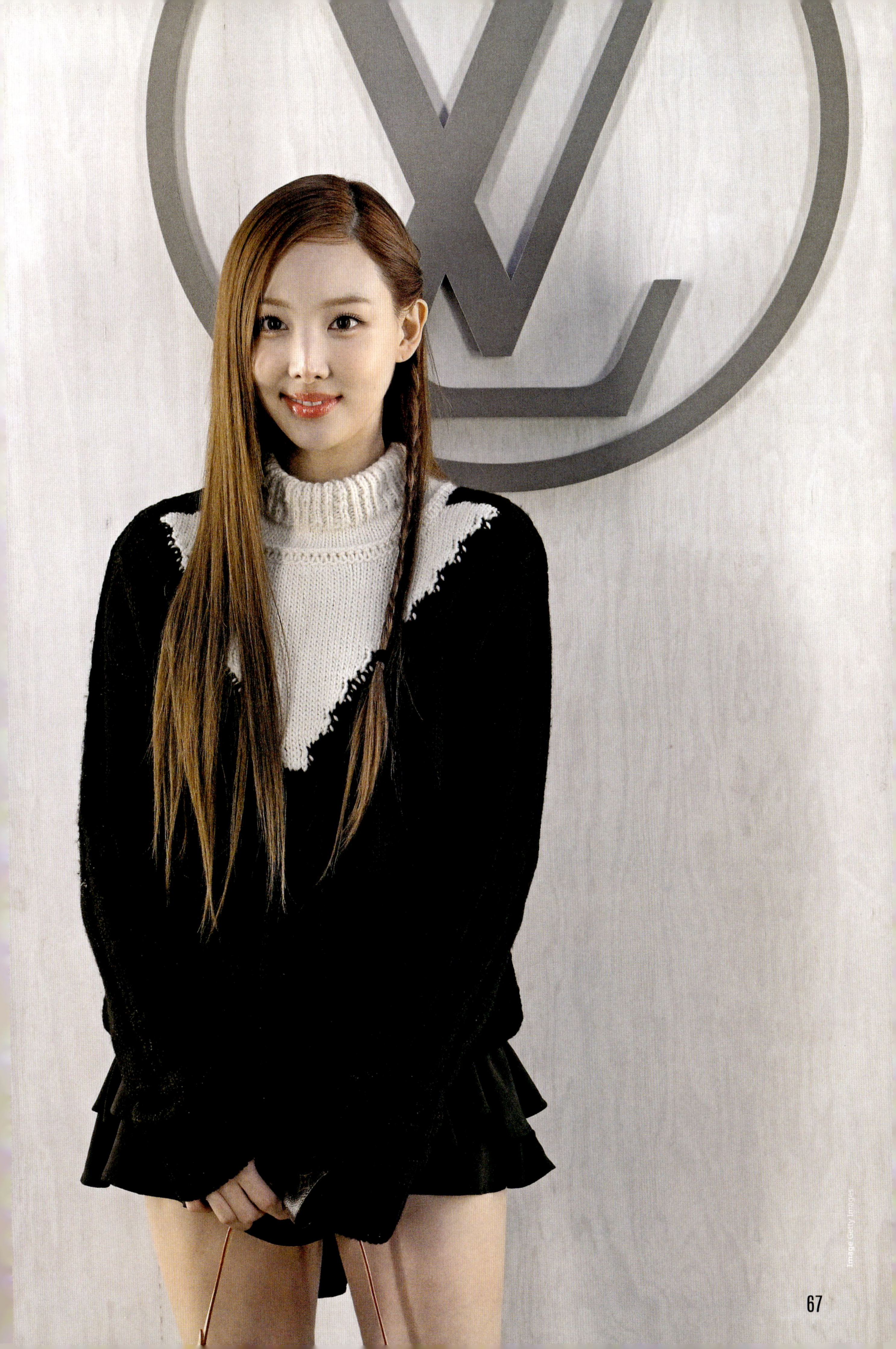

Image Getty Images

ULTIMATE FAN'S GUIDE TO TWICE

Between 1&2

TWICE's eleventh EP was called *BETWEEN 1&2*, released 26 August 2022. The seven track EP features the leading single 'Talk That Talk'. Chaeyoung, Dahyun and Jihyo all wrote lyrics for tracks on the EP, with Jihyo credited as a composer on 'Trouble'. The track 'Brave' is an ode to TWICE's fandom, ONCE. The EP surpassed 1 million pre-orders before its release, which made TWICE the third female K-pop group to do so alongside BLACKPINK and æspa. The EP debuted at number three on the *Billboard* 200 in the US. *BETWEEN 1&2* charted across the world and became the sixth best-selling album in 2022.

"The EP surpassed 1 million pre-orders before its release, which cemented TWICE as a major K-pop group alongside artists like Blackpink"

ULTIMATE FAN'S GUIDE TO **TWICE**

"The group performed the song 'MOONLIGHT SUNRISE' to an audience of ONCE, including the self-confessed member of the fan club, Sabrina Carpenter herself"

Billboard Women in Music

In 2023, TWICE won the award for the breakthrough artist at the 2023 *Billboard* Women in Music event, where they were presented the award by Sabrina Carpenter. On 1 March 2023, the group performed the song 'MOONLIGHT SUNRISE' to an audience of ONCE, including the self-confessed member of the fan club, Sabrina Carpenter herself. The group have received a number of big awards over the years, including a number of MAMA awards from 2015 to 2024, and *Billboard* music awards in 2023 including top K-pop Album and top global K-pop Artist and as well as being named on the Forbes 30 Under 30 list in 2020.

ULTIMATE FAN'S GUIDE TO **TWICE**

READY TO BE

TWICE's twelfth EP *READY TO BE* was released on 10 March 2023, just over a week after they received their award at the *Billboard* Women in Music event. 'Set Me Free' is the lead single of seven tracks. NME gave the EP four out of five stars, praising its retro sound, whilst Rolling Stone gave *READY TO BE* a positive rating for its compelling set of songs. Fans adored the tracks across the world, with over 1.7 million pre-order sales breaking TWICE's previous record. The EP made the highest first week vinyl sales in the US for a female group since 1991 – no small thing.

"The EP made the highest first week vinyl sales in the US for a female group since 1991"

ULTIMATE FAN'S GUIDE TO TWICE

MiSaMo's long-awaited debut

On 26 July 2023, MiSaMo released their debut EP, *Masterpiece*, through the label Warner Japan. The members Momo, Sana, and Mina first released 'Bouquet' in January 2023 for the TV series *Liaison: Children's Heart Clinic*, which was to be one of seven tracks on the debut EP. The lead single was chosen to be 'Do Not Touch', written by JYP and Mayu Wakisaka about boundaries in relationships. The members of MiSaMo all wrote lyrics on the EP, across 'Funny Valentine'; 'It's Not Easy for You'; and 'Rewind You'. *Masterpiece* debuted at number one on the Oricon Albums Chart in Japan.

"The lead single was chosen to be 'Do Not Touch', written by JYP and Mayu Wakisaka about boundaries in relationships"

ULTIMATE FAN'S GUIDE TO TWICE

"*The lead single, 'Killin' Me Good' was once again written by JYP, about a passionate relationship and break up*"

Jihyo goes solo

On 18 August 2023, Jihyo branched out herself to release her debut EP, *ZONE*. The lead single, 'Killin' Me Good' was once again written by JYP, about a passionate relationship and break up. Jihyo's debut EP features elements of Latin; R&B and dance pop. American rapper 24kGoldn features on the EP in the dance-pop song 'Talkin' About It', and 'Don't Wanna Go Back' is a duet with the South Korean singer Heize. *ZONE* was a record breaking hit, debuting at number one on the Circle Album Chart – the highest initial sales for a K-pop female soloist in the chart's history.

ULTIMATE FAN'S GUIDE TO **TWICE**

With YOU-th

TWICE's thirteenth EP, *With YOU-th*, was released on 23 February 2024. 'One Spark' is the hit leading single of the six-track EP, which also includes the group's third English-language song, 'I Got You'. 'I Got You' is another ode to the ONCE fanbase, who often come up thematically on TWICE's EPs, demonstrating a strong bond between artist and audience. Chaeyoung noted that the EP was representative of the friendship between the members of TWICE and their youth. This EP marks TWICE's biggest in the US yet, as it hit number one on the *Billboard* 200, making it the third album by a K-pop female group to do so.

"Chaeyoung noted that the EP was representative of the friendship between the members of TWICE and their youth"

ULTIMATE FAN'S GUIDE TO TWICE

Nayeon's solo return

On 14 June 2024, Nayeon returned with a second EP, *Na*. After the last EP's success, Nayeon's solo return was hotly anticipated, and she did not disappoint on the latest seven-track EP. The lead single 'ABCD' is a hip-hop track that showcases a mature side to Nayeon, which is what she has endeavoured to do on this latest EP. Nayeon announced in *Cosmopolitan* that the new EP has a sporty and sexy feel, and presented a challenge her as she experimented with new dance styles. The EP peaked at number one on the Circle Chart, as well as hitting number seven on the *Billboard* 200 chart in the US.

"The lead single 'ABCD' is a hip-hop track that showcases a mature side to Nayeon"

Ultimate Fan's Guide to
TWICE

Future PLC Quay House, The Ambury, Bath, BA1 1UA

Editorial
Editor **Jessica Leggett**
Senior Designer **Harriet Knight**
Head of Art & Design **Greg Whitaker**
Editorial Director **Jon White**
Managing Director **Grainne McKenna**

Contributors
Kate Waldock

Cover images
Getty Images

Photography
Getty Images, Alamy
All copyrights and trademarks are recognised and respected

Advertising
Media packs are available on request
Commercial Director **Clare Dove**

International
Head of Print Licensing **Rachel Shaw**
licensing@futurenet.com
www.futurecontenthub.com

Circulation
Head of Newstrade **Tim Mathers**

Production
Head of Production **Mark Constance**
Production Project Manager **Matthew Eglinton**
Advertising Production Manager **Joanne Crosby**
Digital Editions Controller **Jason Hudson**
Production Managers **Keely Miller, Nola Cokely, Vivienne Calvert, Fran Twentyman**

Printed in the UK

Distributed by Marketforce – www.marketforce.co.uk
For enquiries, please email: mfcommunications@futurenet.com

Ultimate Fan's Guide to TWICE First Edition (MUB6327)
© 2024 Future Publishing Limited

We are committed to only using magazine paper which is derived from responsibly managed, certified forestry and chlorine-free manufacture. The paper in this bookazine was sourced and produced from sustainable managed forests, conforming to strict environmental and socioeconomic standards.

All contents © 2024 Future Publishing Limited or published under licence. All rights reserved. No part of this magazine may be used, stored, transmitted or reproduced in any way without the prior written permission of the publisher. Future Publishing Limited (company number 2008885) is registered in England and Wales. Registered office: Quay House, The Ambury, Bath BA1 1UA. All information contained in this publication is for information only and is, as far as we are aware, correct at the time of going to press. Future cannot accept any responsibility for errors or inaccuracies in such information. You are advised to contact manufacturers and retailers directly with regard to the price of products/services referred to in this publication. Apps and websites mentioned in this publication are not under our control. We are not responsible for their contents or any other changes or updates to them. This magazine is fully independent and not affiliated in any way with the companies mentioned herein.

FUTURE Connectors. Creators. Experience Makers.

Future plc is a public company quoted on the London Stock Exchange (symbol: FUTR)
www.futureplc.com

Chief Executive Officer **Jon Steinberg**
Non-Executive Chairman **Richard Huntingford**
Chief Financial and Strategy Officer **Penny Ladkin-Brand**

Tel +44 (0)1225 442 244

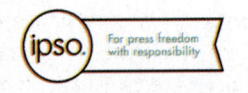